## About this book:

Written in the 24 hours which followed the author losing a sizeable sum at the casino, this warts n all journal takes you back through the eyes of a child to the start of a gambling journey.

It reaches its conclusion today – the first gamble free day of the rest of my life.


If you need help with gambling, then Google "gamble help."

Gamblers Anonymous is a great place to start.


Good luck on your journey.

Thank you

Tye Red

# Contents:

1: A little less conversation

Growing up fell into two main stages moly coddled and then abandoned.

There is no criticism here of either parent or other family member. Shit happens and you fight or flight. You're a victim or a survivor. You find solace or you find distraction, or you find compulsion and addiction.

Abandonment can be self-induced and if self is an ever-present doubting voice on your shoulder enticing distraction, then that voice started to infiltrate my mind from an early age.

Adolescence also allowed me to consider the future and that was never, for me, a happy thought process because it brought about my demise.

A human being aware of their mortality and unable to process or deal with this was a sitting duck for addiction.

The first time I gambled was certainly not with my own money. A pity, looking back, as perhaps the annoyance of losing might have helped me grasp the insanity of going back.

No proof therein though as gamblers always go back – it just made it easier as a child when funds were handed over for the pokies machine on board the annual cross channel ferry to France from my father.

Back then the pokies were a simple affair – one win line and one goal to match three symbols – cherries for a small win and bars or 7's for a higher return. You might even have recollection of a tiny win for getting just one cherry on the win line!

They even had an arm you pulled to begin each spin – the traditional (much loved!) 'One armed bandit' – bandit indeed!

The development of these machines, the technological advances in 40 years that kept the appeal and found ways to inject the endorphin raising chemical highs that made it so appealing are something to behold for the average punter – something to cause untold pain to anyone unable to walk away.

Of course – I could walk away at first. The ferry docked in Calais and the holiday began. As I grew old enough to use my own money so the ease to gamble became a hunt for a win and the games really began.

'A little less conversation' because conversation was replaced with gambling.

As a child, conversations only gave brief highs when my interjection caused laughter or interest.

I was always noted as the only family member who could make nan smile or always had something funny to say.

Even then I doubted the sincerity of reactions and it was certainly hard work to keep the audience entertained.

Highs from pokies machines might have required an injection of funding but highs they were, and they were very addictive and on tap.

Machines started to appeal to the inner mathematician. Holds were offered up to keep two winning symbols in line with the promise of a third hold bringing all three symbols into line. Not everyone knew about this quirk- surely this would give me an advantage?!

Sadly not. As is true now and was a very long time ago now – I couldn't walk away!

Then machine developers created games within games, a cash win could be exchanged for an interactive pursuit for greater funds.

Add music and flashing lights and it was akin to an injection of caffeine or worse.

These games within games were often cat and mouse chases with dangers and defeat determined by the roll of a die.

Sometimes entry into these games was determined by numbers on the winning symbol in a row.

A higher number gave an entry with an extra life – think of that! You knew you were safe from an early exit, a net for a tight rope walker – let's do this and I did!

Game developers quickly caught on and I remember finding my favourite machines in the arcades of an Essex sea-side resort, be they 'The Pink Panther' or 'Monopoly' themed.

I just didn't want to leave the machine.

2: The £10 pint

When I was old enough to go to the pub for a drink, I was old enough to spend more time gambling.

Each pub had two or three slot machines and if I wasn't on one, I was watching the person on it.

It's a bit like going to the pub when your favourite sports team are playing continuously on the big screen. You're not going to get the positive social interactions so pivotal in the teenage years when all you are doing is looking elsewhere and wanting to be elsewhere.

So, I'd order a pint and ask for the
change in coins – machines didn't take
notes then – that little advance would
have me inserting $100 bills decades
later, in the blink of an eye!

The coins would go in, often with a
friend or two in tow to make it a
longer experience and one not so
anti-social.

We'd develop the phrase 'squids in'
for the pound coins deposited into the
hungry jaws of the pokie machine.

Friends would have their financial limit and then myself and a fellow sufferer mate could consider continuing to feed the beast, often only doing so together to prevent the other from having a win if allowed to play alone.

I worked at a pub for a while and witnessed these machines being emptied by the company who provided them to the landlord – they made thousands each week, now they make thousands each day and yet the buzz of a win made them irresistible, and I was becoming powerless to say no.

### 3: Crossing the line

Although the visits to the pub were evidence that I couldn't be in the same room as one of these machines without wishing to play on it, I had not yet become a full-blown addict, but my behaviour was certainly not helping my inner growth.

My college years were spent in arcades and cafes – the UK had pokie machines everywhere!

I never saved money, although I had a part time job.

Watching others gamble made me envious of their wins. It became a thing to monitor another player and step in as they left dejected with the insane belief that their loss made you winning, more likely.

The only thing that was more likely was the speed of depositing coins and the pressing of autoplay to make the endorphin hits all that more rapid.

So, when did I cross the line?

That invisible line was crossed with the invention of the internet.

As quickly as you could say 'Ask Jeeves' there were online casinos.

The slow initial speed of the internet meant CD Roms would be sent out to you to give you speedier access and faster gameplay.

Online gaming meant credit card or debit card details to fund a transfer.

Whereas before, you were restricted by how much money you'd taken out for the night, now the only restriction was how much money your bank account had, or your credit card allowed.

Betting companies quickly understood that a punter's compulsive behaviour could be used to their advantage by providing one button speedier re-funding.

One press of a computer mouse meant the previous deposit was repeated.

At this time wins took days to appear in your account so any attempt to keep tabs (no pun intended) were not something a compulsive gambler could do.

One favourite gambling machine in the café, pub, arcade or casino was overnight replaced with hundreds of online machines – imagine that to a drug user. The overnight legalising and unlimited supply of all opioids – happy days. A daze indeed.

The continual development of technology means these machines have developed like their older cousins.

Bonus games that offer the chance of large wins – wins large enough to claw back losses or fund the next bet but oh so clever!

Bonus games repeat so that you might get two or three in quick succession, imagine the buzz, despite ridiculously low payouts sometimes, and then none for hours.

So, then the designers of these games must have cottoned on that the bonus games were such a draw that they created a pay up front purchase to go straight to the bonus game, rather than waiting for chance to step in.

The way these worked was that you'd pay say fifty times a normal game credit to leap straight to the bonus game.

But sometimes the bonus games, even with maximum stake at play (we'll get to that in a minute!) would pay a pittance, repeat, repeat, repeat!

Chasing losses rather than seeking a big win are what most gamblers are pursuing if you see one in action. A 50c game will not get your money back quickly but a $10 one might. I have happily spent over a $1000 to feel the joy or relief of an $800 win.

Inevitably, though, the $800 would
then be 'reinvested!'

Politicians under pressure from the
anti – gambling lobby, most prevalent
in minority governments, have
introduced a few safeguards in some
countries.

These include the use of a payment
card to control a spend or limiting the
cost of each spin.

Teaching children of the dangers of
any compulsive, escape behaviour
hold out a better beacon of hope for
the future.

Sporting affiliations seeking a quick injection of cash will often give in to the gambling lobby for sponsorship and moral codes are understandably not what drives their financial futures.

Despite messages akin to those appearing on the backs of cigarettes putting reality into view – "you lose more than you win" - the compulsive gambler is powerless.

Once they're hooked then there is not much they can do, not if they are fighting this illness alone.

4: Kenny Rogers
<u>________</u>


Imagine the scenario, you go to the casino or begin to gamble online (there are plenty of gambling blockers here if this online pariah is causing irreparable damage.)


Anyway, you enter the casino, go on a machine and score an unlikely minor or major jackpot in an early spin – scoring you somewhere between $400 and $1500. What do you do?


Well Kenny Rogers in his song 'The Gambler' advocates that you should know, "when to walk away and know when to run!"

Despite his song being focused on card players, the same is of course true for any form of gambling – if you win, get the hell out of there!

A person who is not a compulsive gambler would take a photo of their win and head to the cashier's desk to cash out before switching to a penny machine or roulette wheel for a bit more 'harmless' fun.

A compulsive gambler, on the other hand, does not publicise his or her win as it is future funding for a later bet and often that later bet is an immediate one at a much higher stake.

You see a gambler with a win is a gambler who wants to win even more.

The machine showing $1200 to collect to a compulsive gambler is saying in their minds spend $200 of that on a higher stake in case the machine is ready to pay out more.

Yes $200 punted just like that – half a week's shopping, the internet and tv channels for a month, two tanks of petrol – you get the picture!

Inevitably the $1200 becomes $1000 in the wink of an eye and then the loss must be chased, the endorphin hit must happen again at all costs.

A gambler can lose a lot of money
very quickly.

$10 a spin equates to $3000 in an
hour – a family holiday!

I've won big in my time, mostly online
where the companies set withdrawal
rules meaning that much of your
winnings sit ready to use for a further
punt, as only a certain amount can be
sent back to your bank each week.

Do I have the self-control to set a daily
budget and await the money in my
account – I'm an addict – of course
not.

I am powerless over my gambling, I know "when to walk away and when to run." I just don't, won't or can't.

<u>5: Systems</u>

The best system is not to gamble and to not have access to any money.

I've tried having spending money in one pocket and keeping winnings in the other and seeing how I have done by the end of the night.

I've tried taking my partner with me – when she is turned away, I insert a higher denomination note.

I've tried leaving my credit card in the car... bit ridiculous that one!

An acquaintance informed me that he bet on a colour in roulette and doubled his stake but retained his choice after each unsuccessful spin.

I watched the casino await his cash withdrawal ahead of a 12th unsuccessful spin of the wheel!

There is judgement and form in some gambling. But it is mainly luck and in my chosen 'field of expertise' (cough!) it is entirely luck.

I'm a fairly intelligent being and yet I trust my family's future, my own future on **luck!**

Gamblers who cannot or will not stop are liars and losers in life.

I remember a gentleman, new to Gamblers Anonymous who stopped the meeting mid therapy and told us sheepishly that he'd have to leave the room. As the room looked on, he admitted he had come to GA under the mistaken impression that we discussed systems to become better gamblers!

Gamblers anonymous is accurately described in my group as "the winners circle!"

The organisation of meetings varies around the globe, but each is guided by a twelve-step program that is shared by other addictive associations AA, NA and the like.

Step 1: I am powerless over gambling.

This is the hardest step to crack and every opportunity to have a bet, if abstinence is not in place, will lead to further and pitiful demoralisation.

So here I am writing a book about my experiences throwing money away because, despite periods of not gambling, the urge has just not gone away.

Step 12 (the final step) reads, "having made an effort to practise these principals in all our daily affairs, we tried to carry this message to other compulsive gamblers."

If in a small way I am lighting a pathway for a compulsive gambler to seek help or showing the reality of our plight to a family member or friend or colleague beset with knowing one, then this was worthwhile.

It is a selfish recovery program but less selfish than not joining it!

All the steps in-between Steps 1 and 12 are about taking responsibility for what damage you have done and seeking forgiveness from those whose lives you have tarnished.

Also, there is mention of asking a higher power for help to repair character defects.

I've always thought of this as a bit of a chicken and egg scenario.

Which came first the compulsive gambler or the character defect?

Did I gamble to escape from my character defects (in my case anxiety) or did gambling create or worsen these traits?

What I know for certain, is that these faults cannot be addressed whilst still in full gambling mode.

The 'winner's circle' has those who have been inside jail, inside hospitals or inside divorce courts. Those who appear each week have sanity and wisdom. Those who drift away usually reoffend and get worse.

6: Track record

There are some compulsive gamblers who get the message to stop at the first time of asking.

Whether their exhausted life partner or parents brought them into the rooms of GA, or if they stumbled in after reaching rock bottom, they got it.

They stopped and they began their recovery.

They continued to take their medication (attending meetings) and years or decades later they still practice steps 1 and 12 every time they give a therapy.

For me, I have had periods of abstinence, six years, four years, eighteen months. I have continued to hold the family purse strings – big mistake and I have drifted in and out of meetings.

WHY?

Am I lazy?

Do I resent those who now have happier lives?

I always resented the person on the machine next to me enjoying a win that they won't 'reinvest!'

Do I feel that I am not a loser requiring help?

Am I in denial?

The answer lies squarely in the power of the addiction and the insane yet oft repeated belief that, "this time it will be different."

"I will go with a budget."

"I will only gamble for a limited time."

"If I win, I will walk (run?) away."

"I will not withdrawal any more money once I am out of cash."

"I won't need an online gambling block – I have the ability to avoid temptation"


"I can be trusted with money."


BULLSHIT!

The line that I crossed decades ago –
for me, the onset of online gambling,
was a one-way street, there is no
turning back there is no other
direction of travel.


If you put me next to a gambling
device and I have money in my hand I
will have a bet and I won't stop until
my money has gone with my sanity
once more beaten to a pulp.


If you are a compulsive gambler and
are considering a bet, then remember
your track record. It will not change. It
cannot improve but it can certainly
get worse!

<u>7 Meetings make it</u>

At your GA meeting you will announce your date of last bet and get an opportunity to discuss your week and your progress both in abstinence and in addressing elements of the 12-step program.

The main point is to listen.

I am a little over celebrating milestones (badges and pizzas at 6 months and then yearly) as my own experience (if nothing else) teaches me that any struggle is best confronted and thus celebrated "a day at a time."

Gamblers Anonymous is a selfish program – you only turn up in the first place to help yourself.

Over time, you gain solace and improved sanity because people in the room understand you better than anyone else in your life.

That can make it intimidating – if you are a private person or shy then speaking aloud and baring your soul is not easy.

Though it's got more chance of success that what you were doing before you walked into a meeting.

Keeping going to meetings and seeing the same faces and hearing the same therapies can lead to familiarity breeding a form of contempt.

It's probably the gambler inside looking for reasons to skip the next meeting and history tells us that not attending meetings leads you back to gambling.

To put it simply, everyone in the "winners circle" usually hasn't had a bet that day. You're in the right place!

Moreover, each week or couple of weeks a returning member or a new member walk in the door and without realising it they are delivering Step twelve to the room.

Their recent heartache and pain are universally understood in the room and serve as a reminder of the old life currently behind us.

Members finish each meeting with the serenity prayer and many groups add the saying:

"Keep coming back it works!"

Whatever you hear or say in a meeting will have been experienced by another; nothing, **repeat** nothing, that you say can surprise them.

The numbers present belie the massive problems gambling causes – the room is the tip of an iceberg, but it will keep your head above water – if you show up.

8: The Serenity Prayer

The meetings mention a "higher power."  This can be a finding or rediscovery of a God (of your own understanding.)

Most addicts in recovery put their success down to being present at meetings and in trying to rebuild shattered relationships, egos and lives. Meetings are their "higher power."

In search of accepting what life throws at you, without the need to use addiction to hideaway, simply ask of YOUR higher power:

"God, grant me the serenity to accept the things I cannot change, the courage to change the things I can and the wisdom to know the difference."


And yes…

"Keep coming back – it works!"